Exploring the Mind

A Comprehensive Introduction to Psychology

Freudian Trips

Copyright Page

Published by Omniterra Media Inc

First Edition

Visit the author's website at www.freudiantrips.com

Disclaimer

The views and opinions expressed in this book are those of the author(s) and do not necessarily reflect the official policy or position of any other agency, organization, employer, or company. The contents of this book are for informational and educational purposes only and are not intended to serve as professional advice, diagnosis, or treatment.

The information provided in this book is believed to be accurate and reliable as of the date of publication. However, it may include some errors or inaccuracies, and no warranty or guarantee is provided regarding the accuracy, timeliness, or applicability of the content.

Readers are encouraged to consult with professional philosophers, educators, or other qualified professionals where appropriate for personalized advice. The author(s) and publisher shall not be liable for any loss, damage, or harm caused or alleged to be caused, directly or indirectly, by the information or ideas contained, suggested, or referenced in this book.

By reading this book, the reader acknowledges and agrees that they are solely responsible for how they interpret and apply the information contained herein.

This book may also include references to other works, studies, and sources. These references are provided for further reading and exploration and do not imply endorsement or validation of the specific theories, viewpoints, or interpretations presented in those works.

Preface

Why Psychology Matters

Imagine you're in a bustling café, sipping on your favorite drink. You observe a group of teenagers laughing at a shared joke, a couple deep in a serious conversation, and a barista calling out orders, wearing a smile that doesn't quite reach her eyes. These everyday scenes might seem ordinary, but beneath the surface, there's a complex interplay of emotions, thoughts, and behaviors. That's where psychology comes in.

Psychology is the study of the mind and behavior. It helps us understand why we think, feel, and act the way we do. Have you ever wondered why certain songs make you emotional? Or why you instantly like some people and not others? Or why certain scents can trigger powerful memories? The answers to these questions and countless others lie in psychology.

The relevance of psychology extends beyond personal introspection. It plays a pivotal role in our societies, shaping everything from the advertisements we see to the way businesses operate and even how laws are formulated. Understanding psychology can improve our relationships, make us more effective communicators, and enhance our decision-making abilities.

In essence, psychology matters because it is the key to understanding ourselves and the world around us.

The Goals of this Book

Now that we've established the significance of psychology, you might wonder, "What can I expect to gain from this book?" Here's what we aim to achieve:

Demystifying Psychology: By the end of this book, the term 'psychology' won't be just a fancy word. You'll have a grasp of its essence, its branches, and its applications.

Bridging the Gap: While there are many scholarly texts on psychology, this book aims to bridge the gap between complex psychological concepts and everyday understanding. Think of this as your friendly guide to the world of the mind.

Real-world Applications: Ever wanted to improve your communication skills or make better decisions? We'll dive into practical applications of psychology that you can use in your daily life.

A Glimpse into the Future: As with all fields, psychology is evolving. We'll give you a sneak peek into where psychology is headed, with emerging trends and the role of technology.

Fueling Curiosity: This isn't just a passive read. We hope to ignite a spark of curiosity in you, encouraging you to delve deeper into this fascinating field.

In the chapters that follow, we'll embark on a journey, delving deep into the human mind. Whether you're a student, a professional, or simply someone curious about why humans do what they do, there's something in here for everyone. So, buckle up and get ready to explore the intricate maze that is the human psyche!

Chapter I: Introduction - The Roots of Psychology

The Origins of Psychology: A Historical Overview

Imagine a time when the mysteries of the human mind were attributed to the whims of gods or the alignment of stars. A time when dreams were considered messages from the divine, and mental illnesses were seen as curses or possession. It might sound like a plot from an ancient myth, but that's how our ancestors once perceived the world.

As humans evolved, so did our curiosity. We began to ask questions about our own nature: Why do we dream? What causes our emotions? How do we learn and remember?

To find answers, early civilizations turned to philosophy. Great thinkers like Socrates, Plato, and Aristotle pondered the nature of thought and behavior. They laid the groundwork with their discussions on memory, learning, motivation, and emotion.

Fast forward to the Renaissance, a period of great revival in art, culture, and science. The human mind and its capacities became a subject of fascination. Artists like Leonardo da Vinci tried to unravel the mystery of human anatomy and, by extension, the human mind.

However, it was only in the late 19th century that psychology emerged as a distinct scientific discipline. Wilhelm Wundt, often regarded as the father of modern psychology, established the first laboratory dedicated to psychological research in 1879 in Leipzig, Germany. This marked the beginning of psychology's journey from philosophical discussions to experimental studies.

Since then, the field of psychology has grown and diversified, branching out into various areas, each exploring different facets of the human experience.

Understanding the Term: 'Psychology'

Let's break down the word: 'Psychology'. It comes from two Greek words - 'Psyche', which means 'soul' or 'mind', and 'Logos', which means 'study' or 'knowledge'. So, at its core, psychology is the 'study of the mind'.

But, what does studying the mind entail?

Imagine your mind as a vast ocean. On the surface, you have waves of thoughts, emotions, and behaviors that are visible and evident. Dive deeper, and you'll find currents of memories, desires, and fears. Go even deeper, and there's a bedrock of unconscious motives, deep-seated beliefs, and instincts.

Psychology ventures into this vast ocean, exploring everything from the fleeting surface waves to the mysterious depths below. It seeks to understand how we perceive the world, how we learn and grow, why we feel certain emotions, and why we behave the way we do.

To sum it up, the roots of psychology are deep-seated in our history, drawing from philosophy, biology, and even the arts. As we journey through this book, we'll unravel the intricate tapestry of the human mind, understanding its wonders and complexities. Whether you're diving into the realm of psychology for the first time or revisiting it, there's always something new to discover. So, let's set sail on this voyage of self-discovery!

Chapter II: Exploring the Branches of Psychology

Psychology is a vast field with diverse areas of study. To better understand this landscape, let's examine some of the major branches:

Clinical Psychology: The Diagnosticians

Imagine you're in a cozy office, speaking to a therapist. As you describe your experiences, she listens intently, aiming to assess mental health concerns. This is the domain of clinical psychology.

Clinical psychologists assess, diagnose, and treat mental, emotional, and behavioral disorders. Through psychotherapy and other interventions, they work to improve emotional wellbeing and daily functioning. Their invaluable work provides relief to countless people.

Cognitive Psychology: The Mind Decoders

Picture yourself focused intently on a math problem, or trying to interpret abstract art. Cognitive psychologists study these complex thought processes, from attention and memory to perception, thinking and language.

These "mind detectives" use experiments to uncover the hidden workings behind how we acquire, process and store information. Their findings help reveal the mechanisms of the enigmatic human mind.

Social Psychology: Of Two Minds

Imagine yourself influenced by peer pressure, or changing your beliefs to fit into a group. Social psychologists investigate how our thoughts, feelings, and behaviors are shaped by others.

Studying interactions from romance to rivalry, this field explores how we perceive ourselves and others. The insights unlocked have far-reaching implications for society.

Many More Branches

While we have only highlighted a few, psychology contains a multitude of other fascinating branches. Forensic psychology applies psychological principles to criminal investigations. Developmental psychology studies how we grow and change through life. Evolutionary psychology examines how human behavior is influenced by evolution. And the list goes on.

Psychology's diverse fields provide multifaceted lenses into the human psyche. Together, they help fulfill the overarching goals of psychology: to describe, understand, predict and influence behavior. This ever-growing knowledge aids both human flourishing and scientific advancement.

Chapter III: Psychology vs. Psychiatry: The Crucial Differences

In the vast ocean of mental health and well-being, two terms often float to the surface: psychology and psychiatry. While they might sound similar and indeed share common goals, they approach mental health from different angles. Think of them as two sides of the same coin, each unique and essential in its own right.

The Role of a Psychologist

Imagine you have a puzzle, a beautiful picture of your mind, made of many pieces. Sometimes, these pieces get jumbled, and you can't quite make sense of the image. Enter the psychologist.

The Puzzle Guide: Psychologists are like guides who help you piece together the puzzle of your mind. They hold expertise in understanding human behavior, thoughts, and emotions.

Talk It Out: One primary tool psychologists use is 'talk therapy' or counseling. Through conversations, they help individuals understand their feelings, overcome emotional challenges, and make positive changes in their lives.

Diverse Techniques: Not all puzzles are the same. Psychologists use a variety of therapeutic techniques, tailored to the individual's needs. This could range from cognitive-behavioral therapy, which focuses on changing negative thought patterns, to family therapy, which addresses family dynamics.

It's worth noting that while psychologists understand the intricacies of the human mind, they typically don't prescribe medication. That's where psychiatrists come in.

The Role of a Psychiatrist

Imagine your mind as a complex machine, with gears, levers, and circuits. Sometimes, there might be a glitch—a gear that doesn't turn as it should or a circuit that misfires. Psychiatrists are the mechanics of the mental world.

Medical Experts: Psychiatrists are medical doctors who specialize in mental health. They possess a deep understanding of the physical and mental aspects of psychological issues.

Prescription Power: One of the key differences between psychologists and psychiatrists is the ability to prescribe medication. If a mental health concern is due to a chemical imbalance in the brain, a psychiatrist can recommend medicine to help correct it.

Holistic View: Psychiatrists don't just focus on medication. They also provide psychotherapy, counseling, and other treatments, ensuring a comprehensive approach to mental health.

To wrap it up, think of psychologists and psychiatrists as teammates working towards the common goal of mental well-being. A psychologist delves deep into the mind's labyrinth, guiding individuals through their emotions and thoughts. On the other hand, a psychiatrist brings a medical perspective, addressing the biological aspects of mental health.

Whether you're seeking understanding, healing, or both, it's essential to know which professional to turn to. As you journey further into the world of psychology, remember that mental health is multifaceted, and each facet has its own expert ready to help.

Chapter IV: The Far-Reaching Applications of Psychology

Psychology has invaluable applications in diverse areas of life. Let's explore some of the key realms it impacts:

Harnessing Psychology in Business

Imagine you're a marketing executive trying to sell a new product. To craft an effective campaign, you'll need to understand what motivates consumer behavior. This is where business psychology comes in.

By leveraging insights into emotions, cognition and social influence, professionals can boost marketing, streamline organizations and enhance workplace culture. Understanding psychology is crucial for organizational success.

The Role of Psychology in Education

Picture a classroom where a teacher uses praise and rewards to motivate students. Or an advisor who helps teens choose career paths suited to their personalities. These demonstrate applications of educational psychology.

This field aims to understand how people learn and retain information at different ages. These findings help develop effective teaching methods, curricula and assessments. When applied properly, psychology has immense potential to improve educational outcomes.

Psychology in Law Enforcement

Imagine police interrogating a suspect or witnesses identifying a perpetrator from a line-up. Here, law enforcement uses psychology to investigate crimes.

Forensic psychologists assist with case investigations, offender profiling and interviewing techniques. Their expertise helps extract information to exonerate the innocent and convict the guilty. Psychology is a powerful tool for justice.

Enhancing Personal Growth

Whether understanding your own emotions, improving relationships or relieving stress, psychological knowledge can profoundly enrich your personal life. Practices like meditation, self-reflection and therapy have roots in psychology.

Applied wisely, psychology helps us know ourselves more deeply in order to live more fulfilling lives. In essence, psychology empowers personal growth and well-being.

In diverse fields from business to law enforcement, psychology has real-world impacts. Its principles and insights have tremendous potential to improve human life on both individual and societal levels.

potential to improve human life on both individual and societal levels.

Chapter V: Major Theoretical Approaches in Psychology

Have you ever gazed at the sky on a clear night and marveled at the constellations? Each star, though different, contributes to a broader pattern, painting a unique story in the night sky. Similarly, the vast field of psychology is illuminated by various theories, each shedding light on a different aspect of the human mind and behavior. Let's embark on a journey through some of these bright stars.

A. Psychoanalytic Theory of Sigmund Freud

The Iceberg Metaphor

Imagine an iceberg floating in the ocean. A small portion is visible above the water, while the vast majority remains submerged beneath. This is how Sigmund Freud, an Austrian neurologist, envisioned the human mind.

Conscious Mind (The Tip): This is the part we're aware of—our current thoughts, feelings, and perceptions.

Preconscious (Just Below the Surface): Information that we aren't actively thinking of but can easily bring to awareness, like a childhood memory.

Unconscious (Deep Below): a storehouse of memories, urges, and sentiments that we are not consciously aware of. Freud thought that this aspect had a significant impact on our emotions and conduct.

Freud suggested that our early childhood experiences, particularly with our parents, shape our personalities and behaviors as adults. He emphasized the role of internal conflicts and unconscious desires in driving human behavior.

B. Behavioral Theories of B.F. Skinner

The Laboratory of Life

Have you ever trained a pet or celebrated a child's good behavior with a treat? If so, you've applied the principles of behavioral theory without even realizing it!

B.F. Skinner, an American psychologist, believed that all behaviors are learned through interaction with the environment. He introduced the concept of 'operant conditioning', which is essentially learning from the consequences of our actions.

Rewards and Punishments: According to Skinner, actions that result in positive reinforcement (such as praise or treats) are more likely to be repeated than those that result in negative reinforcement (such as reprimanding).

Through this lens, behavior is shaped and molded by the environment, making us products of our experiences.

C. Humanistic Approach of Carl Rogers

The Blooming Flower

Imagine a seed. Given the right amount of sunlight, water, and care, it blossoms into a beautiful flower. Carl Rogers, an influential American psychologist, viewed humans in a similar light.

Rogers felt that people have intrinsic kindness and potential. People can develop and reach their full potential if they are given the correct environment, one that is characterized by compassion, acceptance, and understanding.

At the heart of this theory is the idea of 'self-actualization', which is the process of realizing and expressing one's capabilities and creativity.

D. Other Theories: An Overview

The universe of psychological theories doesn't end here. There are several other approaches, each offering a unique perspective:

Cognitive Theory: Focuses on how we think, learn, and remember.

Biological Theory: Explores how brain functions, genes, and hormones influence our behavior.

Evolutionary Theory: Examines how our ancestral past and the process of natural selection shape our behaviors today.

In conclusion, just as a night sky is illuminated by countless stars, the realm of psychology is enriched by diverse theories. Each theory, with its unique perspective, helps us understand the intricate tapestry of the human mind and behavior. As you continue your journey through psychology, remember that understanding these theories is like having a map of the stars, guiding you through the vast expanse of the human psyche.

Chapter VI: Revealing Hidden Dimensions of Behavior

Human behavior and mentality often contain subtle complexities beneath the surface. Let's explore some key psychological insights that reveal deeper dimensions:

The Trickery of Optical Illusions

Picture yourself looking at an optical illusion, where static lines seem to move before your eyes. These illusions expose the hidden mechanisms behind visual perception.

Perception is an intricate psychological process, influenced by both optical data and the brain's interpretive faculties. Studying optical illusions and other perceptual phenomena helps unravel the science behind how we see and interpret the world.

Decoding the Dynamics of Groups

Now imagine yourself in a large crowd moved by a shared purpose. Or in a team where members bond through cooperation. These demonstrate the powerful psychological influences of group dynamics.

This field investigates how groups form, attract members, and impact behavior. The insights uncovered have profound implications for society, helping us understand conformity, aggression, leadership, and more.

Psychology's Role in Mental Health

Picture a therapist helping a patient manage anxiety. Or a researcher studying how childhood trauma affects brain development. These exemplify psychology's crucial role in mental health.

By studying factors involved in emotional distress and wellbeing, psychology advances our understanding of mental illness. Its findings help develop more effective diagnoses, treatments and prevention methods. Psychology plays an integral part in both treating and de-stigmatizing mental health issues.

From optical illusions to group think, psychology sheds light on hidden aspects of our minds and behavior. Continued research will further unravel the mysteries of the human psyche and its intricacies.

Chapter VII: Psychology in Action - Real-World Applications

Have you ever noticed how certain colors can uplift your mood, while a song from your past can flood you with nostalgia? Or perhaps, wondered why some advertisements just stick in your mind? Welcome to the world of psychology in action!

Our daily lives are filled with countless moments where psychology plays a silent yet powerful role. Let's dive into some of these real-world applications and discover the magic behind the mundane.

A. Using Psychology to Improve Communication

The Art of Listening and Speaking

Imagine you're painting a picture. The colors you choose, the strokes you make, all convey a message. Similarly, communication is an art, and psychology is the palette that colors it.

Empathy is Key: Ever felt instantly connected to someone because they just "get" you? That's empathy in action. By understanding and sharing another person's feelings, we can foster deeper connections.

The Power of Body Language: Did you know that a lot of our communication is non-verbal? A simple smile, a raised eyebrow, or folded arms can speak volumes. Being aware of these subtle cues can greatly enhance our communication skills.

B. The Role of Psychology in Decision-Making

The Crossroads of Choice

Life is a series of choices - from deciding what to wear in the morning to choosing a career path. But what influences these decisions?

Emotions and Choices: Have you ever made a hasty decision when you were upset, only to regret it later? Our emotions can significantly influence our choices. Recognizing and understanding these emotional triggers can lead to better decision-making.

Group Think: Sometimes, being in a group can sway our decisions. Knowing when to stand firm and when to be flexible is a delicate balance that psychology can help navigate.

C. Stress Management through Psychological Techniques

The Calming Oasis in the Chaos

In today's fast-paced world, stress seems like an unwelcome companion for many. But what if we told you that with the help of psychology, you could find pockets of calm amidst the chaos?

Mindfulness and Meditation: Imagine floating on a calm sea, the gentle waves lulling you into a state of peace. That's the power of mindfulness and meditation. By focusing on the present moment, we can distance ourselves from the whirlwind of worries and stress.

The 'Me Time' Principle: Sometimes, all we need is a break. Engaging in activities we love, like reading, gardening, or even just taking a walk, can act as a psychological balm, reducing stress and rejuvenating us.

In essence, psychology isn't just limited to therapy rooms or textbooks. It's interwoven into our daily lives, influencing our actions, choices, and interactions. Recognizing and harnessing this can lead to improved relationships, better decision-making, and an overall enriched life experience. So, the next time you're faced with a dilemma, or just need a moment of calm, remember - psychology's got your back!

Chapter VIII: The Evolving Landscape of Psychology

Like all sciences, psychology continues to grow and change over time. What might the future look like for this fascinating field? Let's examine some emerging directions:

New Branches on the Horizon

Picture social media users interacting in the virtual world. Or artificial intelligences created to mimic human cognition. Exploring new phenomena like these may spur novel branches of psychology.

Some potential emerging fields include internet psychology, exploring online behavior, and machine psychology, studying artificial intelligence minds. Psychology must constantly expand and adapt to address new realities of human existence.

Technology's Expanding Role

Now imagine researchers using virtual reality to assess responses to stressful situations. Or mining social media data to study behavioral trends across cultures.

Technologies like AI, neuroimaging and digital analytics provide new tools to gather psychological insights. As technology progresses, it will enable more precise measurement of behavior, advanced experimentation and complex data analysis. The psychology of the future could integrate both human skills and technological tools.

While new branches and methodologies will emerge, psychology's core spirit of inquiry into human nature will remain. Its evolution over the coming decades will depend on the creativity and innovation of researchers asking novel questions about behavior and the mind. As long as mysteries of the human psyche persist, psychology will continue to grow as a field. The only true constant is that our understanding of ourselves and our world will keep expanding.

Chapter IX: Conclusion - The Journey Ahead

As we stand at the edge of this enlightening journey through the mesmerizing world of psychology, it's a bit like reaching a viewpoint after a long hike. From this vantage point, we can look back at the trail we've traversed, appreciate the vistas we've witnessed, and gaze ahead at the many paths still waiting to be explored.

A. Recap and Takeaways

A Tapestry of Insights

Over the course of this book:

We've delved into the very origins of psychology, tracing its roots from ancient philosophical musings to the rigorous science it is today.

We've distinguished between related fields, like psychology and psychiatry, understanding their unique and interconnected roles in mental health.

Through various theories, we've unlocked the doors of the mind, understanding its intricate workings from the perspectives of legends like Freud, Skinner, and Rogers.

We've seen how psychology isn't just theory; it's very much alive and pulsating in our everyday lives, influencing our communication, decisions, and well-being.

Our key takeaway? Psychology isn't just about disorders or therapies. It's about understanding ourselves, the people around us, and the intricate dance of thoughts, emotions, and behaviors that make us uniquely human.

B. Encouraging Further Study

The Horizon Beckons

While we've covered a lot, the realm of psychology is vast and ever-evolving. There are still countless mysteries of the mind waiting to be unraveled and numerous pathways of knowledge yet to be trodden.

If this journey has ignited a spark of curiosity within you:

Dive Deeper: Pick up specialized books, attend lectures, or enroll in courses. There's a treasure trove of knowledge out there, waiting to be discovered.

Join the Conversation: Engage with communities, both online and offline, that share a passion for psychology. The exchange of ideas can lead to profound insights.

Apply It: Remember, psychology is as practical as it is theoretical. Use the insights you've gained to improve your personal and professional life, and to foster deeper connections with those around you.

In conclusion, our expedition through psychology might be drawing to an end, but the journey of discovery never truly ends. With each step, with each question, we come closer to understanding the marvel that is the human mind. So, as you move forward, carry the torch of curiosity brightly, and let the wonders of psychology illuminate your path. Here's to the journey ahead! Safe travels, intrepid explorer!

Chapter X: Glossary of Key Terms

Navigating the world of psychology can sometimes feel like walking through a garden filled with unfamiliar plants. Each term and concept is like a unique flower, waiting to be understood and appreciated. In this chapter, we've curated a bouquet of key terms, presented in simple, everyday language, to help you better grasp the essence of psychology.

1. Behavior: Simply put, it's what we do—our actions, reactions, and everything in between.

2. Cognitive: This is all about thinking. When we talk about cognitive processes, we're referring to things like learning, remembering, problem-solving, and daydreaming.

3. Consciousness: It's the state of being aware—knowing what's happening around you and inside your head.

4. Emotion: Feelings! Whether it's joy, sadness, anger, or surprise, it's how we respond to different situations and experiences.

5. Motivation: The driving force behind our actions. It's what pushes us to work hard, chase dreams, or even just get out of bed in the morning.

6. Perception: How we see, hear, and understand the world around us. It's like the lens through which we view our environment.

7. Personality: The unique blend of traits, habits, and behaviors that make us who we are.

8. Stress: A feeling of tension or strain, often in response to challenging situations. It's like the body's alarm system telling us something needs attention.

9. Therapy: A process where individuals work with trained professionals to understand and address personal challenges or concerns.

10. Unconscious: The part of our mind that holds thoughts, memories, and desires that we're not immediately aware of. Think of it as the hidden storage room of our mind.

While this is just a starting point, it offers a foundational understanding of some of the core concepts in psychology. As you delve deeper into this fascinating realm, you'll encounter many more terms and ideas. But remember, behind every "technical" term is a simple idea, waiting to be understood. Happy exploring!

About Freudian Trips

Welcome to Freudian Trips, your dedicated platform for diving deep into the world of psychology. We are more than just a YouTube channel or a book publisher. We are a beacon of enlightenment, making complex psychological concepts accessible and engaging for all.

Our YouTube channel is a rich repository of psychology made simple. We take the profound and often complex ideas from the world of psychology and break them down into digestible, easy-to-understand content. From the foundational theories of Freud to the cognitive insights of Piaget, we cover a broad spectrum of psychological schools and thoughts, making psychology accessible to everyone, regardless of their background or prior knowledge.

As a book publisher, we take the same approach, transforming intricate psychological theories into comprehensible narratives. Our books are not just collections of words, but vessels of wisdom that make psychology approachable and relatable. We believe that psychology should not be confined to academic circles, but should be available to all who seek to understand the human mind and behavior.

At Freudian Trips, we believe in the power of curiosity and the pursuit of knowledge. We are here to stoke the fires of your curiosity, to guide you on your intellectual journey, and to help you navigate the fascinating world of psychology.

If you are someone who is not afraid to question, to explore, and to learn, then you are in the right place. Join us on this journey of exploration, as we make psychology easy to understand, one concept at a time.

Be sure to visit our Youtube channel at: www.freudiantrips.com/youtube

You can also visit us on the web at www.freudiantrips.com

Welcome to The Freudian Trip community. Stay curious. Stay enlightened.